It's Father's Day!

BY MADDIE SPALDING

The Child's World®
childsworld.com

Published by The Child's World®
1980 Lookout Drive • Mankato, MN 56003-1705
800-599-READ • www.childsworld.com

Photographs ©: iStockphoto, cover, 1, 4, 7, 8, 10–11, 14; Anurak Pong/iStockphoto, 13; Monkey Business Images/iStockphoto, 16–17, 20; ESB Professional/Shutterstock Images, 18–19; Red Line Editorial, 22

ISBN 9781503823808
LCCN 2017944875

Printed in the United States of America
PA02358

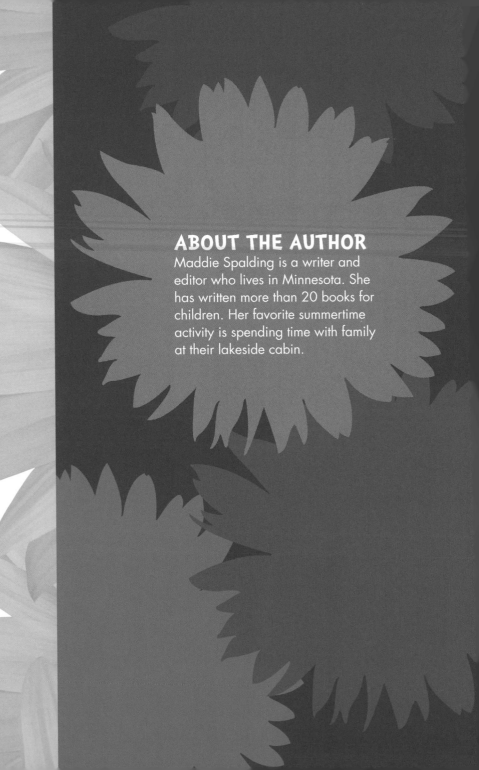

ABOUT THE AUTHOR
Maddie Spalding is a writer and editor who lives in Minnesota. She has written more than 20 books for children. Her favorite summertime activity is spending time with family at their lakeside cabin.

Contents

Father's Day

Today is Father's Day.

I love my Dad!

Father's Day is in June.

It is a special **holiday**.

We show Dad how much

we care.

Gifts

We make cards for Dad.
Dad likes our handmade
cards!

We make art for
Dad. We get him
a gift.

We do **chores**.

We help Dad.

13

14

A Special Day

We let Dad sleep late.

Dads work very hard!

We go out for **brunch**. We get Dad's favorite foods.

My Dad likes sports. We
go to the park. We play
baseball.

We **visit** uncles and grandfathers. Do you celebrate Father's Day?

Handprint Art

Make special handprint art for Father's Day!

Supplies:

paint   white paper
paper plates   markers
paintbrush

Instructions:

1. Pick out your favorite paint colors.
   Squirt each color onto a paper plate.

2. Dab your paintbrush into the paint. Paint the palm of your hand
   with any colors or design you would like, such as stripes.

3. Spread out your hand. Place your palm onto the white paper.
   Let the paint dry.

4. Use the markers to draw designs onto your handprint.

Glossary

brunch—(BRUNCH) Brunch is a meal between breakfast and lunch. We take Dad out for brunch on Father's Day.

chores—(CHORS) Chores are jobs you have to do often. We do chores around the house.

holiday—(HAH-li-day) A holiday is a day when people celebrate a special occasion. Father's Day is a holiday.

visit—(VIZ-it) To visit is to go see other places or people. We visit our family on Father's Day.

To Learn More

Books

Heinrichs, Ann. *Father's Day*. Mankato, MN: The Child's World, 2014.

Kinney, Ada. *Happy Father's Day!* New York, NY: PowerKids Press, 2017.

Web Sites

Visit our Web site for links about Father's Day:
childsworld.com/links

Note to Parents, Teachers, and Librarians: We routinely verify our Web links to make sure they are safe and active sites. So encourage your readers to check them out!

Index